Contents

38

52

69

78

Cooking and Baking with

Splenda

No Calorie Sweetener

This collection of great-tasting dishes made with SPLENDA® Sweeteners brings you recipes with fewer calories than their full-sugar counterparts. With SPLENDA® Sweetener Products, it is simple to have sweetness without all the calories and carbohydrates of sugar.

Several SPLENDA® Sweetener Products are available at your favorite store: SPLENDA® No Calorie Sweetener, in granulated and packet forms, and SPLENDA® Sugar Blend.

SPLENDA® NO CALORIE SWEETENER

SPLENDA® No Calorie Sweetener is available as SPLENDA® Granulated Sweetener, which measures and pours like sugar, and SPLENDA® Packets, which provide the sweetness of two teaspoons of sugar in each packet.

SPLENDA® Granulated Sweetener works best to replace sugar's sweetness in recipes such as pie fillings, cheesecakes, sweet sauces, marinades and glazes. It also works well in quick breads, muffins and cookies. However, its cooking properties are different from sugar. Should you wish to adapt your own recipes, the following tips may be helpful.

1. Volume/Height. Sugar contributes volume to many recipes. When baking cakes, switching from 9-inch round pans to 8-inch round pans with 2-inch sides will help achieve a

better rise. You may also try adding ½ cup nonfat dry milk powder and ½ teaspoon of baking soda for every 1 cup of SPLENDA® Granulated Sweetener.

2. Creaming. When creaming butter or margarine with SPLENDA® Granulated Sweetener, your mixture will appear less smooth than with sugar and may separate upon the addition of eggs.

3. Texture. Cookies often rely on brown sugar for their chewy, crunchy texture. Therefore, you may wish to replace only the white granulated sugar in your cookie recipes. In jams, jellies, puddings and custards, sugar lends a thickening quality. With SPLENDA® Granulated Sweetener, these recipes may be slightly thinner.

4. Moistness. Sugar helps to keep baked goods moist. In muffins and quick breads, adding 1 to 2 tablespoons of honey or molasses will provide moistness as well as flavor.

5. Yeast Activation. SPLENDA® Granulated Sweetener will not activate yeast. Maintain at least two teaspoons of sugar in recipes requiring yeast and replace the remaining sugar with SPLENDA® Granulated Sweetener.

6. Browning. Baked goods made with little or no sugar do not brown like recipes made with sugar. To help achieve a golden-brown color when baking with SPLENDA® Granulated

Sweetener, lightly spray the batter or dough with cooking spray just before placing in the oven.

7. Spread. Cookies often rely on sugar to spread. Should you substitute all the sugar for SPLENDA® Granulated Sweetener in your recipe, you may need to flatten your cookies before baking.

8. Bake Time. Recipes made with SPLENDA® Granulated Sweetener may bake more quickly than those with sugar. Check most baked goods for doneness 3 to 5 minutes earlier than the original recipe states; check cakes 7 to 10 minutes before stated bake time.

9. Storage. Baked goods made with SPLENDA® Granulated Sweetener will stay fresh for 24 hours, when stored in an airtight container at room temperature. To keep your baked goods longer, wrap well and freeze.

10. Jam and Jellies. In canning jams and jellies, SPLENDA® Granulated Sweetener does not provide preservative properties. Consult a sugarless canning cookbook or www.splenda.com for directions for incorporating SPLENDA® Granulated Sweetener in jams and jellies.

SPLENDA® SUGAR BLEND

SPLENDA® Sugar Blend is available in a 2-pound bag with the sweetening equivalency of 4 pounds of sugar.

SPLENDA® Sugar Blend is a mix of pure sugar (sucrose) and SPLENDA® Brand Sweetener (sucralose). It provides great functional properties, like sugar's, for your baked goods—like browning, volume, texture and moistness—but used in place of ordinary sugar, has only half the calories and carbohydrates. It is ideal in recipes such as layer cakes, brownies and confections. Simply substitute half a cup of SPLENDA® Sugar Blend for every full cup of sugar required in a recipe.

You can also use SPLENDA® Sugar Blend in beverages, on cereal and fruit, and elsewhere you might use sugar for half the calories and carbohydrates.

Sugar	SPLENDA® Granulated Sweetener "Cup for cup"	SPLENDA® Sugar Blend "Half as much"
1 cup	1 cup	½ cup
¾ cup	¾ cup	6 tablespoons
⅔ cup	⅔ cup	⅓ cup
½ cup	½ cup	¼ cup
⅓ cup	⅓ cup	2 tablespoons + 2 teaspoons
¼ cup	¼ cup	2 tablespoons

Sweet Starts

Delicious ways to begin the day

Golden Pumpkin Loaf

Makes: 16 slices
Prep time: 15 minutes
Bake time: 40 to 45 minutes

Nonstick cooking spray
⅓ cup plain nonfat yogurt
1 tablespoon nonfat sour cream
2 cups pumpkin purée
3 eggs
¼ cup vegetable oil
2½ cups all-purpose flour
¾ cup SPLENDA® No Calorie Sweetener, Granulated
1 tablespoon plus 1 teaspoon baking powder
1 tablespoon pumpkin pie spice
1 cup raisins
¼ cup chopped walnuts

PREHEAT oven to 350°F. Spray 2 (9×5-inch) loaf pans with nonstick cooking spray.

BLEND yogurt, sour cream, pumpkin, eggs and vegetable oil in large bowl. Add flour, SPLENDA® Granulated Sweetener, baking powder and pumpkin pie spice.

STIR, scraping sides of bowl, and mix in raisins and walnuts.

SPREAD batter into prepared pans. Bake 45 to 50 minutes or until toothpick inserted in center comes out clean.

COOL and cut each loaf into 8 slices.

Nutrition Information per Serving	
Serving size: 1 slice	
Calories:	180
Calories from Fat:	50
Total Fat:	6g
Saturated Fat:	1g
Cholesterol:	40mg
Sodium:	140mg
Total Carbohydrate:	28g
Dietary Fiber:	2g
Sugars:	8g
Protein	5g
Exchanges per Serving	
2 Starches, 1 Fat	

Cranberry Sunshine Muffins

Makes: 8 servings
Prep time: *15 minutes*
Bake time: *15 to 20 minutes*

      Butter-flavored cooking spray
1½ cups all-purpose flour
½ cup SPLENDA® No Calorie Sweetener, Granulated
2 teaspoons baking powder
1 teaspoon baking soda
½ teaspoon ground cinnamon
1 cup chopped fresh or frozen cranberries
¼ cup chopped walnuts
½ cup orange juice
¼ cup nonfat sour cream
1 egg or equivalent in egg substitute
1 tablespoon plus 1 teaspoon reduced-calorie margarine

PREHEAT oven to 375°F. Spray 8 muffin pan cups with butter-flavored cooking spray or line with paper liners.

COMBINE flour, SPLENDA® Granulated Sweetener, baking powder, baking soda and cinnamon in a large bowl. Stir in cranberries and walnuts.

COMBINE orange juice, sour cream, egg and margarine in a small bowl. Add liquid mixture to dry mixture. Stir gently just to combine. Evenly spoon batter into prepared muffin cups.

BAKE for 15 to 20 minutes or until toothpick inserted in centers comes out clean. Cool in pan on wire rack for 5 minutes. Remove muffins from pan and continue cooling on wire rack.

HINT: Fill unused muffin cups with water. It protects the muffin pan and ensures even baking.

Nutrition Information per Serving
Serving size: 1 muffin
Calories: 150
Calories from Fat: 35
Total Fat: 4g
Saturated Fat: 0.5g
Cholesterol: 25mg
Sodium: 320mg
Total Carbohydrate: 24g
Dietary Fiber: 1g
Sugars: 4g
Protein: 4g
Exchanges per Serving
1½ Starches, 1 Fat

Oat Bran Pancakes

Makes: 6 servings
Prep time: *10 minutes*
Cook time: *10 minutes*

- 1   cup oat bran hot cereal, uncooked
- ½   cup all-purpose flour
- ¼   cup SPLENDA® No Calorie Sweetener, Granulated
- 1   teaspoon baking powder
- ½   teaspoon baking soda
- ⅛   teaspoon salt
- 2   cups buttermilk
- ¼   cup egg substitute

HEAT nonstick griddle or frying pan over medium to medium-high heat.

COMBINE oat bran, flour, SPLENDA® Granulated Sweetener, baking powder, baking soda and salt in large bowl. Set aside.

BEAT together buttermilk and egg substitute in small bowl with wire whisk. Pour egg mixture over dry ingredients. Stir together until ingredients are just blended and no large dry lumps appear.

POUR about ¼ cup pancake batter onto hot griddle. Cook pancakes until puffed, browned and slightly dry around the edges. Flip over and cook until golden brown.

Nutrition Information per Serving
Serving size: 2 pancakes
Calories: 160
Calories from Fat: 20
Total Fat: 2g
Saturated Fat: 0g
Cholesterol: 5mg
Sodium: 340mg
Total Carbohydrate: 25g
Dietary Fiber: 4g
Sugars: 4g
Protein: 9g
Exchanges per Serving
1 Starch, 1 Fat-Free Milk

French Toast Strata

Makes: 8 servings
Prep time: *15 minutes*
Chill time: *Overnight*
Bake time: *40 to 50 minutes*

	Nonstick cooking spray
⅓	cup SPLENDA® No Calorie Sweetener, Granulated
1	cup egg substitute
⅔	cup skim milk
1	teaspoon vanilla extract
¾	teaspoon maple extract
8	slices cinnamon raisin bread
2	cups apples, peeled, cored and thinly sliced
¼	cup low-fat cream cheese
1	tablespoon SPLENDA® No Calorie Sweetener, Granulated
½	teaspoon ground cinnamon

PREHEAT oven to 350°F. Spray 8×8-inch square pan with nonstick cooking spray.

BLEND ⅓ cup SPLENDA® Granulated Sweetener, egg substitute, milk, vanilla and maple extracts in medium bowl.

TEAR cinnamon raisin bread into small pieces (1×2 inches). Toss bread and sliced apples with egg mixture in bowl. Coat bread evenly and pour into prepared pan.

CUT cream cheese into 8 chunks and place on top of strata. Blend remaining 1 tablespoon SPLENDA® Granulated Sweetener and cinnamon together. Sprinkle over strata. Cover and refrigerate overnight.

BAKE 40 to 50 minutes or until lightly browned and set. Serve immediately.

Nutrition Information per Serving
Serving size: 2×4-inch slice

Calories:	130
Calories from Fat:	25
Total Fat:	. . . . .2.5g
Saturated Fat:	. . . . .1g
Cholesterol:	. . . .<5mg
Sodium:	. . . . .200mg
Total Carbohydrate:	. . . . . . .20g
Dietary Fiber:	. . . . .2g
Sugars:	. . . . .5g
Protein:	. . . . .7g

Exchanges per Serving
½ Fat, 1½ Starches, ½ Fruit

Lemon Poppyseed Muffins

Makes: 18 muffins
Prep time: *20 minutes*
Bake time: *12 to 15 minutes*

2¼	cups cake flour
¾	cup SPLENDA® No Calorie Sweetener, Granulated
¼	cup sugar
¾	cup unsalted butter, softened
½	cup nonfat instant dry milk
2	teaspoons baking powder
¾	teaspoon baking soda
¼	teaspoon salt
¾	cup buttermilk
2	tablespoons fresh lemon juice
2½	tablespoons grated lemon peel
3	eggs
2	teaspoons vanilla extract
2	tablespoons poppyseeds

Nutrition Information per Serving
Serving size: 1 muffin
Calories: 170
Calories from Fat: 80
Total Fat: 9g
Saturated Fat: 5g
Cholesterol: 55mg
Sodium: 170mg
Total Carbohydrate: 17g
Dietary Fiber: 0g
Sugars: 5g
Protein: 4g
Exchanges per Serving
1 Starch, 2 Fats

PREHEAT oven to 350°F. Place 18 paper baking cups in muffin pans. Set aside.

PLACE cake flour, SPLENDA® Granulated Sweetener, sugar and softened unsalted butter in large mixing bowl. Mix on medium speed 1 to 2 minutes with an electric mixer until blended and crumbly.

ADD nonfat dry milk, baking powder, baking soda and salt. Mix on low speed until blended.

BLEND buttermilk, lemon juice, lemon peel, eggs and vanilla in small bowl. Add ⅔ of buttermilk mixture to flour mixture. Mix on medium speed 1 minute. Stop and scrape sides and bottom of bowl. Mix on medium-high speed 45 to 60 seconds. Reduce mixer speed to low and add remaining liquid; blend. Stop mixer and scrape sides and bottom of bowl again. Add poppyseeds. Mix on medium-high speed 30 seconds.

POUR muffin batter into prepared pans. Bake muffins 12 to 15 minutes or until toothpick inserted in center comes out clean.

Low-Fat Bran Muffins

Makes: 12 muffins
Prep time: *10 minutes*
Bake time: *20 to 25 minutes*

- ¼ cup unsweetened applesauce
- 1 egg
- 1½ cups low-fat buttermilk
- 3 tablespoons canola oil
- 2 teaspoons vanilla extract
- ⅛ teaspoon salt
- ¼ cup nonfat instant dry milk
- ¾ cup SPLENDA® No Calorie Sweetener, Granulated
- 1 cup wheat bran, divided
- 1½ cups all-purpose flour
- 1½ teaspoons baking soda
- 1 teaspoon cinnamon
- 2 tablespoons flaxseeds
- 2 tablespoons dried currants or raisins

PREHEAT oven to 350°F. Oil or line muffin pans with paper baking cups.

BLEND applesauce, egg, buttermilk, oil, vanilla, salt, nonfat dry milk, and SPLENDA® Granulated Sweetener together in large mixing bowl, using wire whisk. Reserve 2 tablespoons wheat bran for topping. Add remaining wheat bran, flour, baking soda and cinnamon to applesauce mixture; stir well. Mix in flaxseeds and currants.

FILL muffin cups with batter. Top each cup with sprinkle of wheat bran. Bake 20 to 25 minutes or until toothpick inserted in center comes out clean.

Nutrition Information per Serving
Serving size: 1 muffin

Calories:	150
Calories from Fat:	45
Total Fat:	5g
Saturated Fat:	0.5g
Cholesterol:	20mg
Sodium:	230mg
Total Carbohydrate:	21g
Dietary Fiber:	3g
Sugars:	4g
Protein:	5g

Exchanges per Serving
1½ Starches, 1 Fat

Mixed Berry Jam

Makes: 3 pints
Prep time: *20 minutes*
Cook time: *40 to 50 minutes*

6   cups fresh raspberries
⅓   cup sugar
3   cups fresh strawberries
1½   cups SPLENDA® No Calorie Sweetener, Granulated
1   cup cold water
1   package no-sugar-needed pectin
1   pint blueberries

COMBINE raspberries and sugar in a heavy bottomed pan. Heat over medium-high heat. Boil 10 to 15 minutes, stirring constantly.

MASH strawberries with a fork or potato masher.

ADD SPLENDA® Granulated Sweetener and strawberries to raspberries. Stir constantly and boil over medium-high heat for an additional 10 to 15 minutes.

POUR cold water into a small saucepan. Whisk pectin into water, and let stand 2 to 3 minutes. Allow the pectin to absorb the water.

BOIL water and pectin, then stir into fruit mixture and reduce heat to medium-low. Add blueberries. Simmer and stir for 5 to 6 minutes, until pectin is thoroughly blended with the fruit.

FREEZE in sterile canning jars.

Nutrition Information per Serving	
Serving size: 1 tablespoon	
Calories:	15
Calories from Fat:	0
Total Fat:	0g
Saturated Fat:	0g
Cholesterol:	0mg
Sodium:	5mg
Total Carbohydrate:	3g
Dietary Fiber:	0g
Sugars:	2g
Protein:	0g
Exchanges per Serving	
Free	

Blueberry Corn Muffins

Makes: 10 muffins
Prep time: *10 minutes*
Bake time: *20 to 25 minutes*

	Nonstick cooking spray
1¾	cups all-purpose flour
½	cup yellow cornmeal
1¼	teaspoons baking powder
½	teaspoon baking soda
½	teaspoon salt
¾	cup SPLENDA® No Calorie Sweetener, Granulated
½	cup unsalted butter, softened
⅓	cup egg substitute
2	teaspoons vanilla extract
1	cup buttermilk
1	cup blueberries (frozen or fresh)

PREHEAT oven to 350°F. Spray muffin pan with nonstick cooking spray or line muffin pans with 10 paper baking cups.

BLEND dry ingredients together in medium mixing bowl. Set aside.

BLEND butter in mixing bowl until light and fluffy. Add egg substitute slowly. Scrape sides and continue to mix until butter forms small lumps. Add vanilla and buttermilk. Mix well. Add dry ingredients in 3 batches. Mix well and scrape sides of bowl after each addition.

FOLD blueberries gently into batter. Scoop batter into prepared muffin cups, filling cups to top. Bake 20 to 25 minutes or until toothpick inserted in center comes out clean.

Nutrition Information per Serving	
Serving size: 1 muffin	
Calories	220
Calories from Fat	90
Total Fat	10g
Saturated Fat	6g
Cholesterol	25mg
Sodium	290mg
Total Carbohydrate	26g
Dietary Fiber	2g
Sugars	3g
Protein	5g
Exchanges Per Serving	
1½ Starches, 2 Fats	

Light
Lunches

Go light for mid-day breaks

Cucumber and Onion Salad

Makes: 6 servings
Prep time: *15 minutes*
Chill time: *2 hours*

2½ cups thinly sliced, unpeeled cucumbers (sliced lengthwise)
½ cup peeled and thinly sliced red onion
⅓ cup SPLENDA® No Calorie Sweetener, Granulated
⅓ cup white vinegar
¼ teaspoon salt
⅛ teaspoon black pepper

TOSS cucumbers and onions together in medium, nonreactive bowl. Set aside.

WHISK together remaining ingredients in separate bowl until blended. Pour over cucumbers and onions. Cover and chill 2 hours; stir several times.

NOTE: To quickly slice cucumbers lengthwise, use a mandoline. Or you may slice them into thin disks.

Nutrition Information per Serving	
Serving size: ¾ cup	
Calories:	15
Calories from Fat:	0
Total Fat:	0g
Saturated Fat:	0g
Cholesterol:	0mg
Sodium:	100mg
Total Carbohydrate:	3g
Dietary Fiber:	0g
Sugars:	2g
Protein:	0g
Exchanges per Serving	
Free	

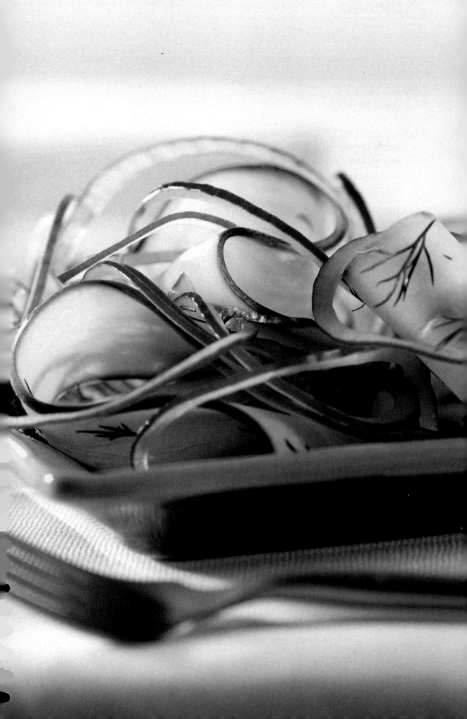

Sweet and Spicy BLT

Makes: 1 sandwich
Prep time: *10 minutes*

Seasoning Mix
  1 tablespoon SPLENDA® No Calorie Sweetener, Granulated
  ¼ teaspoon ground cayenne pepper
  ¼ teaspoon garlic powder
  1 teaspoon paprika

COMBINE all ingredients in small bowl and mix well. Store in an airtight container or storage bag until ready to use.

Makes about 4 servings (1 teaspoon)

Sandwich
  2 slices extra-lean turkey bacon
  1 teaspoon Seasoning Mix (see above)
  2 slices wheat bread
  1 tablespoon fat-free ranch salad dressing
  1 leaf green lettuce
  2 slices fresh tomato

PLACE bacon on microwave-safe pan. Top each slice with ½ teaspoon seasoning mix. Cook bacon in microwave according to package directions.

TOAST bread, then spread with ranch dressing. Layer cooked bacon, lettuce and tomato slices on bread to make sandwich. Serve immediately.

Nutrition Information per Serving
Serving size: 1 sandwich
Calories: 230
Calories from Fat: 70
Total Fat: 7g
Saturated Fat: 1g
Cholesterol: 20mg
Sodium: 820mg
Total Carbohydrate: 31g
Dietary Fiber: 3g
Sugars: 4g
Protein: 9g
Exchanges per Serving
2 Starches, 1 Fat

Layered Chinese Chicken Salad

Makes: 13 servings
Prep time: *45 minutes*
Chill time: *60 minutes*

Dressing
- ½ cup SPLENDA® No Calorie Sweetener, Granulated
- 2 to 3 tablespoons Asian chili garlic paste
- ⅓ cup low-fat mayonnaise
- 3 teaspoons fresh grated gingerroot
- ¼ cup reduced-sodium soy sauce
- ¾ cup rice vinegar
- 1¾ teaspoons cornstarch
- ⅓ cup water

Salad
- 4 boneless, skinless chicken breasts
- 2 bags (12 ounces each) Asian slaw mix or 1 pound shredded napa cabbage
- 1 cup snow peas, trimmed and halved
- 1 can (15 ounces) mandarin oranges, drained
- 2 cups chow mein noodles
- ⅓ cup chopped green onion

Chicken:

MIX SPLENDA® Granulated Sweetener, chili garlic paste, mayonnaise and ginger together in medium bowl. Add soy sauce and rice vinegar; blend.

POUR ¼ cup dressing in zip seal plastic bag. Place chicken breasts in bag, seal and turn to coat. Chill 45 to 60 minutes to marinate.

PLACE remaining dressing in small saucepan. Mix cornstarch and water in small bowl until cornstarch is dissolved. Pour cornstarch mixture into dressing while stirring constantly. Place pan on medium-high heat. Boil 1 to 2 minutes, stirring constantly. Remove dressing from heat and pour into small bowl. Chill 1 hour or until cool.

REMOVE marinated chicken breasts from bag; discard marinade. Grill or broil chicken until internal temperature reaches 160°F. Set aside to cool; slice or shred meat. Cover and refrigerate until ready to assemble salad.

Nutrition Information per Serving	
Serving size: 1 cup	
Calories:	130
Calories from Fat:	40
Total Fat:	3.5g
Saturated Fat:	0.5g
Cholesterol:	20mg
Sodium:	320mg
Total Carbohydrate:	13g
Dietary Fiber:	2g
Sugars:	2g
Protein:	10g

Exchanges per Serving
½ Starch, 1 Lean Meat,
1 Vegetable

Salad:

PLACE 1 bag (6 cups) Asian slaw in straight-sided glass bowl.

Drizzle ⅓ of prepared dressing over slaw. Arrange ½ of prepared chicken and pea pods on top.

ADD remaining slaw to bowl. Top with remaining chicken, oranges and dressing. Chill until ready to serve.

GARNISH with chow mein noodles and green onion before serving.

Options:

Substitute shredded napa cabbage if Asian slaw mix is unavailable. Toasted sliced almonds also make a great garnish. For authentic Asian flavor, add 1 to 2 teaspoons toasted sesame oil.

Raw Broccoli Salad

Makes: 6 servings
Prep time: *5 to 10 minutes*

- 4   cups (about 2 pounds) broccoli florets or broccolini
- ¼   cup minced red onion
- 2   tablespoons SPLENDA® No Calorie Sweetener, Granulated
- 2   tablespoons cider vinegar

Raw Broccoli Salad, continued

2 tablespoons low-fat mayonnaise
2 tablespoons sunflower seeds shelled, roasted and salted
3 tablespoons seedless raisins

CHOP broccoli or broccolini into florets. Set aside.

WHISK together remaining ingredients in medium bowl. Add broccoli. Toss to coat. Chill until ready to serve.

Nutrition Information per Serving
Serving size: ⅔ cup
Calories: 60
Calories from Fat: 30
Total Fat: 2g
Saturated Fat: 0g
Cholesterol: 0mg
Sodium: 60mg
Total Carbohydrate: 9g
Dietary Fiber: 1g
Sugars: 5g
Protein: 2g
Exchanges per Serving
2 Vegetables

Creamy Cole Slaw

Makes: 10 servings
Prep time: *20 minutes*

1½ cups Hellmann's® Low Fat Mayonnaise Dressing*
⅓ cup SPLENDA® No Calorie Sweetener, Granulated
3 tablespoons Vidalia onion (or other sweet onion), finely chopped
2 teaspoons lemon juice
1 tablespoon white wine vinegar
1¼ teaspoons celery seed
¾ teaspoon salt
¼ teaspoon black pepper
8 cups classic cole slaw cabbage mix (1 bag)
½ cup carrots, cut into matchsticks or shredded

Hellmann's® is a registered trademark of Best Foods

Nutrition Information per Serving
Serving size: 2.5 ounces
Calories: 50
Calories from Fat: 14
Total Fat: 1.5g
Saturated Fat: 0g
Cholesterol: 0mg
Sodium: 330mg
Total Carbohydrate: 9g
Dietary Fiber: 1g
Protein: 1g
Exchanges per Serving
2 Vegetables

WHISK all ingredients except cabbage mix and carrots in large bowl.
ADD cole slaw mix and carrots.
REFRIGERATE at least 2 hours. Mix and serve cold.

Orange-Almond Salad

Makes: 4 servings
Prep time: *15 minutes*

- **3** cups assorted salad greens
- **2** navel oranges, peeled and separated into sections
- **½** cup thinly sliced celery
- **2** tablespoons chopped green onion
- **¼** cup cider vinegar
- **¼** cup SPLENDA® No Calorie Sweetener, Granulated
- **2** teaspoons vegetable oil
- **¼** cup toasted slivered almonds

COMBINE greens, orange sections, celery and green onion in large bowl. Set aside.

BLEND vinegar, SPLENDA® Granulated Sweetener and vegetable oil in small bowl. Whisk until smooth. Drizzle dressing mixture evenly over greens mixture. Toss gently to coat.

PORTION salad evenly among 4 plates, about 1¼ cups per plate. Sprinkle 1 scant tablespoon slivered almonds over each serving. Serve immediately.

Nutrition Information per Serving
Serving size: 1¼ cups
Calories: 120
Calories from Fat: 60
Total Fat: 6g
Saturated Fat: 0.5g
Cholesterol: 0mg
Sodium: 25mg
Total Carbohydrate: 16g
Dietary Fiber: 5g
Sugars: 7g
Protein: 3g
Exchanges per Serving
½ Fruit, 1 Vegetable, 1 Fat

Chili, Vegetarian Style

Makes: 16 servings
Prep time: *20 minutes*
Cook time: *30 minutes*

1 tablespoon extra-virgin olive oil
1 jalapeño pepper,* seeded and finely chopped
½ cup chopped onion
1⅓ cups diced red and yellow bell peppers
6 teaspoons chili powder
1½ teaspoons paprika
¼ teaspoon garlic powder
¾ teaspoon ground red pepper
⅓ cup SPLENDA® No Calorie Sweetener, Granulated
3 tablespoons cider vinegar
1 can (28 ounces) crushed tomatoes
2 cans (15 ounces each) black beans, undrained
2 cans (15 ounces each) dark red kidney beans, undrained
1 can (15 ounces) cannellini or other beans, undrained
1 box (10 ounces) frozen corn kernels
Salt

Jalepeño peppers can sting and irritate the skin; wear rubber gloves when handling peppers and do not touch the eyes.

HEAT olive oil in large stock pot. Sauté jalapeño, onion and bell peppers over medium heat until onions are translucent, about 5 to 8 minutes.

ADD remaining ingredients, and season to taste with salt. Bring to boil, cover and simmer over low heat for 20 minutes. Serve hot.**

NOTE: Make ahead for best flavor. For spicy chili, increase ground red pepper to 1 teaspoon and increase chili powder to 7 teaspoons.

If sweeter taste is preferred, increase SPLENDA® Granulated Sweetener to ⅔ cup.

Nutrition Information per Serving
Serving size: 1 cup
Calories: 150
Calories from Fat: 20
Total Fat: 2g
Saturated Fat: 0g
Cholesterol: 0mg
Sodium: 590mg
Total Carbohydrate: 27g
Dietary Fiber: 9g
Sugars: 4g
Protein: 8g
Exchanges per Serving
2 Starches

Warm Spinach Salad

Makes: 4 servings
Prep time: *15 minutes*

Salad
- 1 bag (7 ounces) baby spinach greens
- ½ cup nonfat salad croutons

Dressing
- ¼ cup white vinegar
- ¼ cup water
- ¼ cup Dijon mustard
- 3 tablespoons SPLENDA® No Calorie Sweetener, Granulated
- 5 slices turkey bacon
- ¼ cup chopped red onion
- 2 cloves garlic, peeled and minced

PLACE spinach greens in colander. Wash and remove stems; drain well. Place in serving bowl and add croutons.

BLEND vinegar, water, mustard and SPLENDA® Granulated Sweetener. Set aside.

SLICE bacon into small, thin strips. Place in medium saucepan and fry over medium-high heat until crispy, about 3 to 4 minutes.

ADD onion and garlic and cook over medium-high heat 1 to 2 minutes, stirring often.

ADD vinegar mixture and simmer 1 to 2 minutes. Pour over spinach and croutons. Toss well. Serve immediately.

Nutrition Information per Serving
Serving size: 1¾ cups
Calories: 150
Calories from Fat: 30
Total Fat: 3.5g
Saturated Fat: 1g
Cholesterol: 10mg
Sodium: 660mg
Total Carbohydrate: 5g
Dietary Fiber: 5g
Sugars: 1g
Protein: 5g
Exchanges per Serving
1 Fat, 1 Vegetable

Curried Turkey and Apple Salad

Makes: 4 servings
Prep time: *20 minutes*

- 1 tablespoon canola oil
- 1 tablespoon curry powder
- ¼ cup diced onion
- 2 tablespoons fresh lemon juice
- 2 tablespoons SPLENDA® No Calorie Sweetener, Granulated
- ¼ teaspoon salt (optional)
- ½ cup low-fat mayonnaise
- 2 stalks celery, thinly sliced
- 1 pound roasted turkey breast, cut into ½-inch dice
- 1 medium apple, cut into ¼-inch dice
  Salad greens
- ⅓ cup chopped dried apricots, for garnish

HEAT oil in small saucepan over medium-high heat. Add curry powder and onion. Cook and stir 1 to 2 minutes or until onions are tender. Add lemon juice, SPLENDA® Granulated Sweetener and salt. Simmer over medium heat until sauce begins to thicken, about 1 minute. Remove from heat and cool.

STIR mayonnaise into cooled sauce; mix well. Toss together celery, turkey and apple in large bowl. Add dressing and gently toss until evenly coated.

SERVE turkey mixture mounded on salad greens, garnished with chopped apricots, if desired.

Nutrition Information per Serving
Serving size: ¾ cup

Calories:	300
Calories from Fat:	60
Total Fat:	6g
Saturated Fat:	0.5g
Cholesterol:	100mg
Sodium:	360mg
Total Carbohydrate:	24g
Dietary Fiber:	3g
Sugars:	12g
Protein:	35g

Exchanges per Serving
1 Starch, ½ Fruit, 4 Very Lean Meats

Daily
Dinners

Easy enough for weeknights, delicious enough for parties!

Quick Glazed Pork Loin

Makes: 4 servings
Prep time: *10 minutes*
Bake time: *25 to 30 minutes*

1 (1- to 1½-pound) pork
   tenderloin
¼ cup water
2 tablespoons tomato paste
1 tablespoon orange juice
   concentrate
2½ teaspoons chili powder
⅛ teaspoon salt
1 tablespoon SPLENDA®
   No Calorie Sweetener,
   Granulated
1 teaspoon white vinegar
1 package (14 ounces) frozen
   mixed vegetables

PREHEAT oven to 425°F. Rinse pork loin and pat dry. Set aside.

MIX water, tomato paste, orange juice concentrate, chili powder, salt, SPLENDA® Granulated Sweetener and white vinegar in small bowl. Whisk until smooth.

PLACE pork loin in foil-lined 13×9-inch baking pan. Cover with half of glaze. Bake 15 minutes.

REMOVE pork loin from oven. Cover with remaining glaze. Place vegetables around pork loin. Bake an additional 15 minutes or until vegetables are hot and pork loin internal temperature reaches 160°F.

Nutrition Information per Serving Serving size: 3 ounces pork and ½ cup vegetables	
Calories:	180
Calories from Fat:	36
Total Fat:	4g
Saturated Fat:	1.5g
Cholesterol:	75mg
Sodium:	220mg
Total Carbohydrate:	9g
Dietary Fiber:	3g
Sugars:	3g
Protein:	29g

Exchanges per Serving
½ Starch, 5 Very Lean Meats,
1 Vegetable

Baked Salmon
with Orange-Ginger Sauce

Makes: 2 servings
Prep time: *15 minutes*
Bake time: *10 to 15 minutes*

1	(2½-inch) section fresh gingerroot
1	cup orange juice
¼	cup SPLENDA® No Calorie Sweetener, Granulated
2	tablespoons nonfat half-and-half
¼	teaspoon cornstarch
¼	teaspoon salt
2	tablespoons unsalted butter, softened
2	cups frozen stir-fry vegetables
2	salmon filets (10 ounces raw, weight will reduce after baking)

PREHEAT oven to 450°F.

MAKE sauce: Peel gingerroot and slice into 10 slices. Pour orange juice into small saucepan. Add SPLENDA® Granulated Sweetener and gingerroot. Bring to rolling boil over medium-high heat. Boil 10 to 12 minutes or until reduced to 2 to 3 tablespoons. Remove from heat and lift out gingerroot with fork. Set aside.

MIX half-and-half, cornstarch and salt. Whisk softened butter, 1 tablespoon at a time, into orange juice mixture. Stir until melted. Add half-and-half mixture. Stir well. Place saucepan back on heat. Bring to simmer over medium-high heat.

REMOVE sauce from heat and mix in blender 15 to 20 seconds or until smooth and light in color. Set aside.

PREPARE salmon: Place vegetables in oiled 8×8-inch baking pan. Place salmon fillets on vegetables. Bake 10 to 15 minutes or until fully cooked and tender. Place vegetables and salmon on serving plates. Spoon sauce over salmon. Serve with steamed rice, if desired.

Nutrition Information per Serving	
Serving size: 4 ounces salmon and 1 cup vegetables	
Calories:	490
Calories from Fat:	230
Total Fat:	27g
Saturated Fat:	10g
Cholesterol:	120mg
Sodium:	420mg
Total Carbohydrate:	24g
Dietary Fiber:	3g
Sugars:	16g
Protein:	31g
Exchanges per Serving: 4 Lean Meats, 3 Fats, 2 Vegetables, 1 Fruit	

Citrus Glazed Chicken with Toasted Almonds

Makes: 4 servings
Prep time: *15 to 20 minutes*
Bake time: *15 to 20 minutes*

4	boneless, skinless chicken breasts (total 1 pound)
3	tablespoons orange juice concentrate, thawed, divided
2	tablespoons fresh lemon juice
½	cup chicken broth
3	tablespoons SPLENDA® No Calorie Sweetener, Granulated
1½	teaspoons cornstarch
1	tablespoon unsalted butter
1	tablespoon fresh chives, chopped
1	tablespoon fresh parsley, stemmed and chopped
¼	cup sliced almonds, toasted

PREHEAT oven to 425°F. Place chicken breasts on foil-lined baking sheet. Brush with 1 tablespoon orange juice concentrate. Bake 15 to 20 minutes or until cooked through.

PLACE remaining orange juice concentrate, lemon juice and chicken broth in small saucepan. Blend SPLENDA® Granulated Sweetener and cornstarch in small bowl. Stir cornstarch mixture into broth. Heat over medium-high heat and simmer 8 to 10 minutes or until sauce thickens slightly. Remove from heat. Whisk butter into sauce. Add chives and parsley. Pour sauce over chicken breasts. Top with almonds.

SERVE with tossed salad or steamed vegetables.

Nutrition Information per Serving
Serving size: ¼ recipe

Calories:	230
Calories from Fat:	70
Total Fat:	7g
Saturated Fat:	2.5g
Cholesterol:	75mg
Sodium:	190mg
Total Carbohydrate:	9g
Dietary Fiber:	1g
Sugars:	5g
Protein:	28g

Exchanges per Serving
½ Starch, 4 Very Lean Meats, 1 Fat

Lemon Chicken

Makes: 4 servings
Chill time: *10 minutes*
Prep time: *10 to 15 minutes*

2	teaspoons cornstarch, divided
¼	cup low-sodium soy sauce, divided
12	ounces chicken breast tenders, cut in thirds
¼	cup fresh lemon juice
¼	cup fat-free chicken broth
1	teaspoon fresh gingerroot, minced
2	cloves garlic, peeled and minced
1	tablespoon SPLENDA® No Calorie Sweetener, Granulated
1	tablespoon vegetable oil
¼	cup red bell pepper, seeded and sliced
¼	cup green bell pepper, seeded and sliced

MIX 1 teaspoon cornstarch and 1 tablespoon soy sauce in medium bowl. Add sliced chicken tenders. Chill 10 minutes.

STIR lemon juice, remaining soy sauce, chicken broth, ginger, garlic, SPLENDA® Granulated Sweetener and 1 teaspoon cornstarch together in medium bowl to make sauce.

HEAT oil in medium frying pan. Add chicken and cook over medium-high heat for 3 to 4 minutes or until chicken is no longer pink in center. Add lemon sauce and sliced peppers. Cook 2 to 3 minutes more or until sauce thickens and peppers are hot.

SERVE with rice or Asian noodles.

Nutrition Information per Serving
Serving size: 3 ounces chicken, plus peppers and sauce

Calories:	160
Calories from Fat:	40
Total Fat:	4.5g
Saturated Fat:	0.5g
Cholesterol:	50mg
Sodium:	560mg
Total Carbohydrate:	6g
Dietary Fiber:	0g
Sugars:	2g
Protein:	22g

Exchanges per Serving
3 Very Lean Meats, 1 Vegetable, 1 Fat

Chili Meatloaf

Makes: 6 servings
Prep time: *15 minutes*
Bake time: *55 to 60 minutes*

   Nonstick cooking spray
1   cup tomato sauce, divided
3   tablespoons SPLENDA® No Calorie Sweetener, Granulated, divided
2   teaspoons prepared yellow mustard
1½ teaspoons chili powder, divided
1   tablespoon dried onion flakes
1   tablespoon dried parsley flakes
½   teaspoon salt
1   pound extra-lean ground turkey or beef
¼   cup Italian seasoned bread crumbs

PREHEAT oven to 350°F. Spray 9×5-inch loaf pan with nonstick cooking spray.

MIX ⅓ cup tomato sauce, 2 tablespoons SPLENDA® Granulated Sweetener, mustard, 1 teaspoon chili powder, onion flakes, parsley flakes and salt in large mixing bowl. Add ground meat and bread crumbs; stir well. Shape meat mixture into loaf form to fit pan; place in prepared pan.

MIX remaining tomato sauce, chili powder and SPLENDA® Granulated Sweetener together in small bowl. Spoon mixture over top of meat loaf.

BAKE 55 to 60 minutes. Remove meat loaf from oven and place on wire rack. Cool 5 minutes before slicing.

Nutrition Information per Serving	
Serving Size: ⅙ of recipe	
Calories:	120
Calories from Fat:	70
Total Fat:	5g
Saturated Fat:	3g
Cholesterol:	30mg
Sodium:	580mg
Total Carbohydrate:	8g
Dietary Fiber:	1g
Sugars:	2g
Protein:	18g
Exchanges per Serving	
½ Starch, 2 Lean Meats	

Fresh & Fun

Sweet treats with SPLENDA® No Calorie Sweetener

Grandma's Strawberry Shortcakes

Makes: 6 servings
Prep time: *10 to 15 minutes*
Bake time: *7 to 9 minutes*

Butter-flavored cooking spray
6 cups chopped fresh strawberries
¾ cup SPLENDA® No Calorie Sweetener, Granulated
1 cup plus 2 tablespoons reduced-fat biscuit baking mix
⅓ cup fat-free milk
2 tablespoons nonfat sour cream

Nutrition Information per Serving	
Serving size: 1 shortcake plus ¾ cup sauce	
Calories:	160
Calories from Fat:	35
Total Fat:	4g
Saturated Fat:	<1g
Cholesterol:	<1mg
Sodium:	290mg
Total Carbohydrate:	29g
Dietary Fiber:	4g
Protein:	3g
Exchanges per Serving	
1 Starch, 1 Fruit, 1 Fat	

PREHEAT oven to 425°F. Spray a baking sheet with butter-flavored cooking spray.

PLACE 2 cups strawberries in a large bowl. Mash well with fork or potato masher. Stir in ½ cup SPLENDA® Granulated Sweetener. Add remaining 4 cups strawberries. Mix well to combine. Cover and refrigerate.

COMBINE baking mix and remaining ¼ cup SPLENDA® Granulated Sweetener in a medium bowl. Add fat-free milk and sour cream. Mix well until a soft dough forms.

DROP batter by spoonfuls onto prepared baking sheet to form 6 shortcakes. Bake for 7 to 9 minutes or until golden brown. Place baking sheet on a wire rack and let set for 10 minutes.

SERVE each shortcake on a dessert dish and spoon about ¾ cup strawberry sauce over top.

Candied Popcorn

Makes: 10 servings
Prep time: *15 minutes*
Bake time: *20 to 25 minutes*

      Nonstick cooking spray
13   cups freshly popped popcorn
 1   egg white
 2   tablespoons dark molasses
 2   teaspoons vanilla extract
½   teaspoon salt
¾   cup SPLENDA® No Calorie Sweetener, Granulated
½   cup dry roasted peanuts

PREHEAT oven to 325°F. Spray an 11×13-inch pan with nonstick cooking spray and set aside.

PLACE popcorn in large bowl. In small bowl, add egg white, molasses, vanilla, salt and SPLENDA® Granulated Sweetener; whisk well. Add peanuts and stir until peanuts are coated. Pour over popcorn. Toss until popcorn is coated.

PLACE on prepared baking pan. Bake 20 to 25 minutes, stirring occasionally, until mix is crispy. Remove mix from oven and spread onto parchment or waxed paper to cool. Cool to room temperature before serving.

Nutrition Information per Serving
Serving size: 1¼ cups
Calories: 110
Calories from Fat: 35
Total Fat: 4g
Saturated Fat: . . . . : . 1g
Cholesterol: 0mg
Sodium: 240mg
Total Carbohydrate: 15g
Dietary Fiber: 2g
Sugars: 3g
Protein: 3g
Exchanges per Serving
1 Starch, 1 Fat

Summer Berry Terrine

Makes: 8 servings
Prep time: *20 minutes*
Chill time: *45 minutes*

- **4** cups fresh strawberries, sliced
- **1** cup fresh blueberries
- **1** cup fresh raspberries
- **1** envelope unflavored gelatin
- **⅔** cup SPLENDA® No Calorie Sweetener, Granulated
- **⅔** cup water
- **¼** teaspoon vanilla extract
- **¼** cup whipping cream
  Reduced-fat frozen whipped topping and sprigs of fresh mint (optional)

COMBINE first 3 ingredients in a large mixing bowl; toss gently.

SPRINKLE gelatin and SPLENDA® Granulated Sweetener over water in a small saucepan; let stand 1 minute. Cook over low heat, stirring until gelatin dissolves (about 2 minutes). Stir in vanilla. Set aside.

BEAT whipping cream until soft peaks form; set aside.

PLACE saucepan containing gelatin mixture in a bowl of ice water; stir with a rubber spatula until gelatin mixture is the consistency of unbeaten egg white. Remove from ice water; quickly stir in whipped cream. Spoon the cream mixture over berries, tossing gently to coat.

SPOON mixture into a lightly oiled 8-inch loaf pan; cover and chill for 45 minutes or until set. Unmold onto a cutting board and slice into 8 servings. Garnish with reduced-fat whipped topping and mint sprigs, if desired.

Nutrition Information per Serving
Serving size: 1 slice (⅛ terrine)
Calories: 80
Calories from Fat: 30
Total Fat: 3g
Saturated Fat: 1.5g
Cholesterol: 10mg
Sodium: 10mg
Total Carbohydrate: 12g
Dietary Fiber: 3g
Sugars: 7g
Protein: 2g
Exchanges per Serving
1 Fruit, 1 Fat

Tempt Your

Sweet Tooth

Cookies, bars, and pies

SPLENDA® and Spice Cookies

Makes: 30 cookies
Prep time: *10 minutes*
Chill time: *2 hours*
Bake time: *10 to 12 minutes*

6	tablespoons vegetable shortening
6	tablespoons margarine
1	cup SPLENDA® No Calorie Sweetener, Granulated
1	egg
¼	cup molasses
2	cups all-purpose flour, sifted
¾	teaspoon ground ginger
1	teaspoon ground cinnamon
½	teaspoon ground cloves

Nutrition Information per Serving
Serving size: 1 cookie
Calories: 90
Calories from Fat: 45
Total Fat: 5g
Saturated Fat: 2g
Cholesterol: 5mg
Sodium: 30mg
Total Carbohydrate: 9g
Dietary Fiber: 0g
Sugars: 2g
Protein: 1g
Exchanges per Serving
½ Starch, 1 Fat

MIX together shortening, margarine, SPLENDA® Granulated Sweetener, egg and molasses.

SIFT flour, ginger, cinnamon and cloves. Add to shortening mixture and stir to form dough. Wrap dough in plastic wrap. Chill dough in refrigerator until firm, about 2 hours.

PREHEAT oven to 350°F. Form dough into 30 balls (1 heaping teaspoon each). Place cookies on ungreased cookie sheet and pat down gently with fork making criss-cross pattern.

BAKE cookies in center of oven for 10 to 12 minutes. Do not overbake. Cookies will look chewy but become crisp after cooling. Cool cookies on wire cooling rack.

Lemon Raspberry Bars

Makes: 16 (2-inch square) bars
Prep time: *10 minutes*
Bake time: *35 to 45 minutes*
Chill time: *2 hours*

Crust:
　　Butter-flavored cooking spray
¾　cup SPLENDA® No Calorie
　　Sweetener, Granulated
¾　cup all-purpose flour
　　Pinch salt
¼　cup light butter

Filling:
1¼　cups SPLENDA® No Calorie
　　Sweetener, Granulated
2　tablespoons all-purpose flour
½　cup egg substitute
½　cup half-and-half
½　cup fresh lemon juice
1½　tablespoons grated fresh
　　lemon peel
¼　cup fruit-only raspberry
　　preserves

Nutrition Information per Serving Serving size: 1 bar (2-inch square)	
Calories:	70
Calories from Fat:	20
Total Fat:	2.5g
Saturated Fat:	1.5g
Cholesterol:	10mg
Sodium:	45mg
Total Carbohydrate:	12g
Dietary Fiber:	0g
Sugars:	3g
Protein:	2g
Exchanges per Serving	
1 Starch	

PREHEAT oven to 350°F. Spray 8×8-inch baking pan with butter-flavored cooking spray.

MIX SPLENDA® Granulated Sweetener, flour and salt in medium bowl. Cut in light butter until mixture is crumbly. Do not overmix. Press dough into prepared baking pan. Bake 15 to 20 minutes or until lightly browned.

PLACE SPLENDA® Granulated Sweetener and flour in medium bowl. Stir well. Add egg substitute and half-and-half. Stir until blended. Slowly add lemon juice while stirring constantly; add lemon peel. In small bowl, stir raspberry preserves until liquified. Spread evenly over warm crust.

POUR lemon mixture over preserves. Bake 20 to 25 minutes or until set. Remove from oven and allow to cool before chilling.
Chill in refrigerator 2 hours before serving.

Raspberry Cheese Tarts

Makes: 10 servings
Prep time: *25 minutes*
Bake time: *20 minutes*
Chill time: *2 hours*

Crust
1¼ cups graham cracker crumbs
5 tablespoons light margarine
¼ cup SPLENDA® No Calorie Sweetener, Granulated

Filling
4 ounces reduced-fat cream cheese
½ cup plain nonfat yogurt
1 cup SPLENDA® No Calorie Sweetener, Granulated
½ cup egg substitute
1 cup frozen raspberries

Crust:
PREHEAT oven to 350°F. In medium bowl, mix together graham cracker crumbs, margarine and ¼ cup SPLENDA® Granulated Sweetener. Press about 1 tablespoon of crust mixture into 10 muffin pan cups lined with paper liners. Set aside.

Filling:
IN small bowl, beat cream cheese with electric mixer on low speed until soft, about 30 seconds. Add yogurt and beat on low speed until smooth, approximately 1 minute. Stir in SPLENDA® Granulated Sweetener and egg substitute until well blended.

PLACE 1½ tablespoons raspberries (4 to 5) into each muffin cup. Divide filling evenly among muffin cups. Bake for 20 minutes or until firm.

REFRIGERATE for 2 hours before serving. Garnish as desired.

Nutrition Information per Serving	
Serving size: 1 tart	
Calories:	120
Calories from Fat:	45
Total Fat:	5g
Saturated Fat:	2g
Cholesterol:	5mg
Sodium:	160mg
Total Carbohydrate:	15g
Dietary Fiber:	0g
Sugars:	4g
Protein:	4g
Exchanges per Serving	
1 Starch, 1 Fat	

Cheery Cherry Pie

Makes: 8 servings
Prep time: *20 minutes*
Bake time: *40 to 50 minutes*

1	(15-ounce) package refrigerated piecrusts
2	(14.5-ounce) cans pitted tart red cherries, undrained
⅔	cup SPLENDA® No Calorie Sweetener, Granulated
¼	cup cornstarch
2	teaspoons fresh lemon juice
¼	teaspoon almond extract
4	to 5 drops red food coloring (optional)

PREHEAT oven to 375°F.

UNFOLD 1 piecrust; press out fold lines. Fit piecrust into a 9-inch pie plate according to package directions.

DRAIN cherries, reserving 1 cup juice; set fruit aside.

COMBINE SPLENDA® Granulated Sweetener and cornstarch in a medium saucepan; gradually stir reserved juice into SPLENDA® Granulated Sweetener mixture. Cook over medium heat, stirring constantly, until mixture begins to boil. Boil 1 minute, stirring constantly. Remove from heat; stir in lemon juice, almond extract and food coloring, if desired. Fold in reserved cherries; cool slightly. Spoon mixture into pastry shell.

UNFOLD remaining piecrust; press out fold lines. Roll to ⅛-inch thickness. Place over filling; fold edges under and crimp. Cut slits in top to allow steam to escape.

BAKE 40 to 50 minutes or until crust is golden. Cover edges with aluminum foil to prevent over browning, if necessary. Cool on a wire rack 1 hour before serving.

Nutrition Information per Serving
Serving size: 1 slice
Calories: 300
Calories from Fat: 130
Total Fat: 14g
Saturated Fat: 6g
Cholesterol: 10mg
Sodium: 210mg
Total Carbohydrate: 41g
Dietary Fiber: 1g
Sugars: 10g
Protein: 3g
Exchanges per Serving
3 Fruits, 2 Fats

Papa's Pecan Tassies

Makes: 20 pieces
Prep time: *10 to 15 minutes*
Bake time: *20 minutes*

1   refrigerated unbaked 9-inch piecrust
½   cup SPLENDA® No Calorie Sweetener, Granulated
2   tablespoons cornstarch
1   egg or equivalent in egg substitute
¾   cup water
1   tablespoon vanilla extract
½   cup chopped pecans

PREHEAT oven to 350°F.

UNFOLD piecrust. Using a 2½-inch biscuit cutter, cut into 12 circles. Press dough scraps together and cut out 8 more circles for a total of 20 circles. Pat pastry circles into miniature muffin (or tassie) cups. Press to form tarts.

COMBINE SPLENDA® Granulated Sweetener, cornstarch, egg and water in a medium saucepan. Cook over medium heat until mixture thickens and starts to boil, stirring constantly. Remove from heat.

STIR in vanilla extract and pecans. Evenly spoon about 1 tablespoon mixture into each tart.

BAKE for 16 to 20 minutes. Place muffin pans on a wire rack and allow to cool for 10 minutes. Remove tassies from pans and continue cooling on wire rack.

Nutrition Information per Serving
Serving size: 2 pieces
Calories: 160
Calories from Fat: 90
Total Fat: 10g
Saturated Fat: 3g
Cholesterol: 25mg
Sodium: 90mg
Total Carbohydrate: 14g
Dietary Fiber: . . . . <1g
Protein: 2g
Exchanges per Serving
1 Starch, 2 Fats

Tennessee Apple Pie

Makes: 8 servings
Prep time: *20 minutes*
Chill time: *1½ hours*
Bake time: *50 to 60 minutes*

Crust
- ¾ cup ice water
- 1 teaspoon vinegar (white or cider)
- 2 cups all-purpose flour, divided
- 3 tablespoons SPLENDA® No Calorie Sweetener, Granulated
- 7 tablespoons vegetable shortening
- Nonstick cooking spray

Filling
- 7 cups Granny Smith apples, peeled, cored, sliced
- ⅔ cup SPLENDA® No Calorie Sweetener, Granulated
- 3 tablespoons cornstarch
- ¾ teaspoon cinnamon
- ⅛ teaspoon salt

MIX ice water and vinegar in a cup. Place ½ cup flour in bowl, adding vinegar-water mix gradually; whisk well. Combine remaining flour and SPLENDA® Granulated Sweetener in medium bowl. Add shortening, using pastry cutter or two knives to cut in until mixture is crumbly. Gradually add water-flour mixture, adding just enough to bind dough together.

DIVIDE dough in half. Gently pat each half into circle on a floured work surface. Cover circles separately with plastic wrap; chill 30 minutes.

PREHEAT oven to 375°F. Spray 9-inch pie pan with nonstick cooking spray. Set aside.

TOSS filling ingredients together in a large mixing bowl.

ROLL out dough on a lightly floured work surface into a circle 11 inches in diameter. Place in

Nutrition Information per Serving
Serving size: 1 slice
Calories: 290
Calories from Fat: 100
Total Fat: 11g
Saturated Fat: 3g
Cholesterol: 0mg
Sodium: 40mg
Total Carbohydrate: 44g
Dietary Fiber: 4g
Protein: 3g
Exchanges per Serving
1 Starch, 2 Fruits, 2 Fats

prepared pie pan and add filling. Roll out remaining dough and cover filling. Crimp edges together with fingertips or fork. Use fork to prick top crust. Brush crust with milk for more golden, even browning.

BAKE 50 to 60 minutes or until crust is golden. Cool pie at least 1 hour before serving.

Apple Cranberry Pie

Makes: 8 servings
Prep time: *30 minutes*
Bake time: *50 to 60 minutes*

Crust
- ¾ cup ice water
- 1 teaspoon vinegar (white or cider)
- 2 cups all-purpose flour, divided
- 3 tablespoons SPLENDA® No Calorie Sweetener, Granulated
- 7 tablespoons vegetable shortening

Filling
- 1 cup fresh cranberries
- ½ cup SPLENDA® No Calorie Sweetener, Granulated
- 1 tablespoon all-purpose flour
- ½ teaspoon cinnamon
- 4 large Granny Smith apples, peeled, cored and sliced
- Nonstick cooking spray

Crust:

MIX ice water and vinegar in cup. Place ½ cup flour in bowl, adding vinegar-water mix gradually; whisk well. Combine remaining flour and SPLENDA® Granulated Sweetener in medium bowl. Add shortening using pastry cutter or two knives until mixture is crumbly. Gradually add water-flour mixture, adding just enough to bind dough together.

DIVIDE dough in half. Gently pat each half into circle on floured work surface. Cover circles separately with plastic wrap and chill dough 30 minutes.

Filling:

PREHEAT oven to 400°F. Coarsely chop cranberries. Mix all filling ingredients together in medium bowl. Spray 9-inch pie pan with nonstick cooking spray.

ROLL out 1 circle of dough on floured work surface to 11 inches in diameter. Place in prepared pie pan. Place filling in crust in pie pan. Roll remaining crust to 10 inches in diameter and place on top of filling. Crimp and seal edges with fingertips or fork. Use fork to prick top crust. Brush crust with milk for browning.

BAKE 50 to 60 minutes or until crust is golden.

Nutrition Information per Serving	
Serving size: ⅛ pie	
Calories:	270
Calories from Fat:	70
Total Fat:	11g
Saturated Fat:	3g
Cholesterol:	0mg
Sodium:	90mg
Total Carbohydrate:	39g
Dietary Fiber:	3g
Sugars:	10g
Protein:	4g
Exchanges per Serving	
1½ Starches, 1 Fruit, 2 Fats	

Currant and Cornmeal Tea Cookies

Makes: 4½ dozen cookies
Prep time: *20 minutes*
Chill time: *1 hour*
Bake time: *7 to 10 minutes*

- ½ cup light butter, softened
- ¼ cup unsalted butter, softened
- ⅔ cup SPLENDA® No Calorie Sweetener, Granulated
- 1 tablespoon vanilla extract
- ¼ cup egg substitute
- 1 tablespoon grated orange peel
- ¼ cup cornmeal
- 1½ cups all-purpose flour
- 1 teaspoon baking powder
- ½ teaspoon ground cinnamon
- ¼ teaspoon ground nutmeg
- ½ cup currants

PREHEAT oven to 325°F. Oil 18×12-inch cookie sheet or baking pan; set aside.

BLEND butters, SPLENDA® Granulated Sweetener and vanilla extract in medium bowl until creamy. Add egg substitute and orange peel; stir. Add cornmeal, flour, baking powder, cinnamon and nutmeg. Mix with electric mixer on low speed (or by hand) briefly, until dough forms. Do not overmix. Add currants; scrape sides of bowl and stir.

REMOVE dough from bowl and divide in half. Roll each half into log shape about 1-inch in diameter. Wrap in plastic wrap and freeze 1 hour, until dough is firm.

REMOVE dough from freezer, unwrap and discard plastic, and cut logs into ¼-inch slices. Place cookies on prepared cookie sheet. Bake 7 to 10 minutes or until just browned.

Nutrition Information per Serving	
Serving size: 4 cookies	
Calories:	130
Calories from Fat:	60
Total Fat:	7g
Saturated Fat:	3.5g
Cholesterol:	20mg
Sodium:	90mg
Total Carbohydrate:	15g
Dietary Fiber:	1g
Sugars:	1g
Protein:	2g
Exchanges per Serving	
1 Starch, 1 Fat	

Raspberry Heart Cookies

Makes: 18 sandwich cookies
Prep time: *20 minutes*
Chill time: *1 hour*
Bake time: *8 to 10 minutes*

¾ cup unsalted butter, softened
¼ cup light butter, softened
1 cup SPLENDA® No Calorie
    Sweetener, Granulated
1 tablespoon vanilla extract
¼ cup egg substitute
¼ cup water
¾ teaspoon vinegar (white or
    cider)
1½ cups all-purpose flour
1½ cups cake flour
¼ teaspoon salt
1 teaspoon baking powder
3 tablespoons "Powdered Sugar"
    (*see page 93*)
⅓ cup sugar-free raspberry preserves

Nutrition Information per Serving
Serving size: 1 sandwich cookie
Calories: 170
Calories from Fat: 90
Total Fat: 10g
Saturated Fat: 3.5g
Cholesterol: 25mg
Sodium: 85mg
Total Carbohydrate: 19g
Dietary Fiber: 0g
Sugars: 2g
Protein: 2g
Exchanges per Serving
1 Starch, 2 Fats

BLEND together butters, SPLENDA® Granulated Sweetener and vanilla extract in medium bowl. Add egg substitute, water and vinegar; mix. Add flours, salt and baking powder. Mix with electric mixer on low speed (or by hand) until dough is formed. Scrape sides and bottom of bowl.

REMOVE dough from bowl and place on floured work surface. Divide dough in half and round each half into a 1-inch thick flat disk. Wrap each dough portion in plastic wrap; chill 1 hour.

PREHEAT oven to 350°F. Oil 18×12-inch baking pan or cookie sheet.

UNWRAP dough and roll out on floured work surface to ⅛-inch thickness. Cut with large (3×4 inches) heart-shaped cookie cutters. Cut small heart shapes out of the centers of half of cookies (these will top filled cookies). Place cookies on prepared pan.

BAKE 8 to 10 minutes or until lightly browned on bottom. Cool on wire rack.

SPRINKLE "Powdered Sugar" over top layer cookies (with center heart cut-outs). Spread 1 teaspoon raspberry preserves on remaining cookies. Place cookies with cut-outs on top of cookies spread with raspberry preserves.

Crunchewey Cran-Nutty Carrot Cookies

Makes: 4½ dozen cookies
Prep time: *15 minutes*
Bake time: *10 to 11 minutes*

Nonstick cooking spray
3 cups quick-cooking oats
1 cup all-purpose flour
1 teaspoon baking soda
1½ cups SPLENDA® No Calorie Sweetener, Granulated
2 large eggs
½ cup canola oil
1 (8-ounce) can crushed pineapple in juice, undrained
1 cup flaked coconut
1 cup shredded carrots
1 cup dried cranberries
1 cup chopped walnuts
1 teaspoon vanilla extract

PREHEAT oven to 350°F. Lightly spray cookie sheets with nonstick cooking spray.

COMBINE oats, flour and baking soda; set aside.

COMBINE SPLENDA® Granulated Sweetener, eggs and canola oil in a large mixing bowl, stirring until blended. Add pineapple with juice, coconut, carrots, cranberries, walnuts and vanilla, stirring until blended. Add dry ingredients, stirring until blended.

DROP dough by tablespoonfuls, 1½ inches apart, onto prepared cookie sheets.

BAKE 10 to 11 minutes or until lightly browned. Transfer to wire racks to cool.

Nutrition Information per Serving Serving size: 1 cookie	
Calories:	80
Calories from Fat:	40
Total Fat:	4.5g
Saturated Fat:	1g
Cholesterol:	10mg
Sodium:	30mg
Total Carbohydrate:	9g
Dietary Fiber:	1g
Sugars:	3g
Protein:	2g

Exchanges per Serving
½ Starch, 1 Fat

Jeweled Apple Pie

Makes: 8 servings
Prep time: *15 minutes*
Bake time: *55 to 65 minutes*

Piecrust
½ (15-ounce) package refrigerated piecrusts

Streusel Topping
⅓ cup all-purpose flour
2 tablespoons SPLENDA® No Calorie Sweetener, Granulated
2 tablespoons dark brown sugar
½ teaspoon ground cinnamon
¼ teaspoon salt
½ cup uncooked regular oats
¼ cup chopped walnuts
¼ cup unsalted cold butter, cut into ¼-inch slices

Filling
½ cup SPLENDA® No Calorie Sweetener, Granulated
1 tablespoon all-purpose flour
1½ teaspoons ground cinnamon
¼ teaspoon ground nutmeg
¼ teaspoon salt
5 Rome or other cooking apples, peeled and sliced (about 2½ pounds)
⅓ cup dried cranberries
⅓ cup golden raisins
3 tablespoons lemon juice
1 tablespoon orange rind
2 teaspoons lemon rind

PREHEAT oven to 425°F.

PLACE piecrust into a 9-inch pie plate according to package directions; fold edges under and crimp.

Streusel Topping:

COMBINE flour, SPLENDA® Granulated Sweetener, brown sugar, cinnamon and salt; stir in oats and walnuts. Cut butter in with a pastry blender until mixture is crumbly.

Filling:

COMBINE SPLENDA® Granulated Sweetener, flour, cinnamon, nutmeg and salt in a small mixing bowl; set aside.

Nutrition Information per Serving	
Serving size: 1 slice	
Calories:	310
Calories from Fat:	120
Total Fat:	13g
Saturated Fat:	6g
Cholesterol:	20mg
Sodium:	280mg
Total Carbohydrate:	48g
Dietary Fiber:	4g
Sugars:	22g
Protein:	4g
Exchanges per Serving	
2 Starches, 1 Fruit, 2 Fats	

COMBINE apple slices, cranberries, raisins, lemon juice, orange and lemon rind in a large mixing bowl; add SPLENDA® Granulated Sweetener mixture and toss gently. Spoon mixture into prepared piecrust. Top with Streusel Topping.

BAKE for 15 minutes. Reduce heat to 375°F and bake for 40 to 50 additional minutes or until topping is golden brown.

Celebration
Cakes

**Make celebrations special
with SPLENDA® No Calorie Sweetener**

Low-Fat Lime Cheesecake

Makes: 16 servings
Prep time: 20 minute
Bake time: 50 to 60 minutes
Chill time: 6 hours or overnight

Crust:
1¼ cups graham cracker crumbs
 ¼ cup SPLENDA® No Calorie
      Sweetener, Granulated
 3 tablespoons butter, melted

MIX ingredients, and press into
10-inch springform pan.

Filling:
 1 pound cream cheese
 1 pound nonfat cream cheese
1¼ cups SPLENDA® No Calorie
      Sweetener, Granulated
2½ tablespoons fresh lime juice
 2 tablespoons grated lime peel
      Pinch salt
 4 eggs

PREHEAT oven to 350°F.

BEAT cream cheeses and
SPLENDA® Granulated
Sweetener until smooth. Add
fresh lime juice, grated peel and
salt; beat until smooth. Add eggs,

1 at a time, scraping sides of bowl
and beating well after each
addition.

POUR cream cheese filling into
prepared crust and bake 50 to
60 minutes or until slightly firm
to touch. Remove from oven. Let
cool 25 to 30 minutes before
placing in refrigerator. Chill 6
hours or overnight before serving.

Nutrition Information per Serving
Serving size: 1 slice
Calories: 210
Calories from Fat: 130
Total Fat: 14g
Saturated Fat: 8g
Cholesterol: 95mg
Sodium: 340mg
Total Carbohydrate: 10g
Dietary Fiber: 0g
Sugars: 2g
Protein: 8g
Exchanges per Serving
½ Starch, 1 Medium-Fat Meat, 2 Fats

Apple Cheesecake Torte

Makes: 8 servings
Prep time: *15 minutes*
Bake time: *35 minutes*

Crust
⅓ cup SPLENDA® No Calorie Sweetener, Granulated
½ cup butter, softened
½ teaspoon vanilla extract
1 cup all-purpose flour

Filling
1 (8-ounce package) cream cheese, softened
¼ cup SPLENDA® No Calorie Sweetener, Granulated
¼ cup egg substitute
½ teaspoon vanilla extract

Topping
⅓ cup SPLENDA® No Calorie Sweetener, Granulated
½ teaspoon ground cinnamon
4 cups peeled and sliced cooking apples (about 3 large apples)
¼ cup sliced almonds

Crust:

PREHEAT oven to 450°F.

BEAT ⅓ cup SPLENDA® Granulated Sweetener and butter at medium speed with an electric mixer for 2 minutes. Stir in vanilla. Add flour, mixing until blended. Press on bottom and ½-inch up sides of a 9-inch spring form pan. Set aside.

Filling:

BEAT cream cheese and ¼ cup SPLENDA® Granulated Sweetener at medium speed with an electric mixer 2 minutes or until creamy. Add egg substitute

Nutrition Information per Serving
Serving size: 1 slice
Calories: 320
Calories from Fat: 210
Total Fat: 23g
Saturated Fat: 13g
Cholesterol: 60mg
Sodium: 190mg
Total Carbohydrate: 24g
Dietary Fiber: 2g
Sugars: 7g
Protein: 5g
Exchanges per Serving
1½ Starches, 4 Fats

and vanilla, beating until blended. Spoon mixture into prepared pan.

Topping Directions:

COMBINE ⅓ cup SPLENDA® Granulated Sweetener and cinnamon; sprinkle over apple slices, tossing until coated. Arrange apple slices over cream cheese filling. Sprinkle with sliced almonds.

BAKE for 10 minutes; reduce temperature to 400°F and bake an additional 25 minutes. Remove cheesecake from oven; cool in pan on a wire rack. Separate sides from pan by releasing spring. Serve warm.

Delightful

Drinks

Guilt-free sips with SPLENDA® No Calorie Sweetener

Strawberry-Orange Smash

Makes: 4 (8 fluid ounce) servings
Prep time: *5 minutes*

2½   cups frozen, unsweetened strawberries
½   cup SPLENDA® No Calorie Sweetener, Granulated
1   cup calcium-fortified orange juice
¾   cup nonfat plain yogurt
½   teaspoon vanilla extract
¼   cup ice cubes

PLACE all ingredients in blender. Mix on low speed 15 to 20 seconds. Remove lid. Stir well. Cover and blend on medium speed until smooth.

POUR into 4 glasses and serve immediately.

Nutrition Information per Serving Serving size: 8 fluid ounces	
Calories: 100	Sodium: 40mg
Calories from Fat: 0	Total Carbohydrate: 21g
Total Fat: 0g	Dietary Fiber: 2g
Saturated Fat: 0g	Sugars: 14g
Cholesterol: 0mg	Protein: 4g
	Exchanges per Serving
	1½ Fruits

Hot Chocolate

Makes: 2 (8 fluid ounce) servings
Prep time: *10 minutes*

- 2 cups 2% reduced-fat milk
- 8 packets SPLENDA® No Calorie Sweetener
- 3 tablespoons powdered cocoa (preferably Dutch processed)

Garnish:
- ¼ teaspoon cinnamon
- 2 tablespoons reduced-calorie whipped topping

PLACE milk in small saucepan. Mix contents of SPLENDA® Packets and cocoa powder in small bowl. Add to milk and whisk well. Simmer 4 to 5 minutes over medium-low heat until steaming.

POUR mixture into 2 serving cups. Optional garnish: Top each with 1 tablespoon reduced-calorie whipped topping and pinch of ground cinnamon.

Nutrition Information per Serving	
Serving size: 8 fluid ounces	
Calories:	160
Calories from Fat:	50
Total Fat:	6g
Saturated Fat:	3.5g
Cholesterol:	20mg
Sodium:	130mg
Total Carbohydrate:	20g
Dietary Fiber:	3g
Sugars:	12g
Protein:	10g
Exchanges per Serving	
½ Starch, 1 Reduced-Fat Milk	

Banana Raspberry Smoothie

Makes: 2 (8 fluid ounces) servings
Prep time: *15 minutes*
Freeze time: *10 minutes*

1	large ripe banana, sliced
5	packets SPLENDA® No Calorie Sweetener
½	cup 1% low-fat milk
1¼	cups frozen unsweetened raspberries

PLACE sliced banana on plate and freeze for 10 minutes or until slightly firm.

COMBINE all ingredients in blender. Blend on medium speed until smooth. Pour into 2 glasses and serve immediately.

Nutrition Information per Serving
Serving size: 8 fluid ounces
Calories: 110
Calories from Fat: 0
Total Fat: 0g
Saturated Fat: 0g
Cholesterol: 0mg
Sodium: 30mg
Total Carbohydrate: 25g
Dietary Fiber: 4g
Sugars: 19g
Protein: 3g
Exchanges per Serving
1½ Fruits

Elegant Eggnog

Makes: 15 (4 fluid ounce) servings
Prep time: *20 minutes*
Chill time: *5 hours or overnight*

1	cup SPLENDA® No Calorie Sweetener, Granulated
1	tablespoon arrowroot powder or cornstarch
1	teaspoon ground nutmeg
7	egg yolks
4	cups whole milk
2	cups nonfat half-and-half
2	tablespoons vanilla extract

MIX together first 3 ingredients in a large heavy saucepan. Set aside.

WHISK egg yolks; add to SPLENDA® mixture, whisking until blended.

ADD milk slowly while stirring continuously.

COOK over low heat, whisking constantly until temperature reaches 175°F (about 5 to 8 minutes).

REMOVE from heat and blend in half-and-half; cool.

COVER and chill at least 3 hours before serving. Add vanilla extract just before serving. Eggnog will keep 3 days in refrigerator.

*Be sure to cook to 175°F as this temperature kills any bacteria in the egg yolks. You may add 1 teaspoon dark rum per serving for an adult; however, nutrient data will change.

Nutrition Information per Serving
Serving size: ½ cup (4 fluid ounces)

Calories:	100
Calories from Fat:	45
Total Fat:	5g
Saturated Fat:	2g
Cholesterol:	115mg
Sodium:	70mg
Total Carbohydrate:	9g
Dietary Fiber:	0g
Sugars:	6g
Protein:	5g

Exchanges per Serving
1 Reduced-Fat Milk

SPLENDA® Sugar Blend

Sour Cream Pound Cake

Makes: 18 servings
Prep time: *15 minutes*
Bake time: *1 hour and 20 minutes*

3	cups sifted cake flour
1½	cups SPLENDA® Sugar Blend
¼	teaspoon baking soda
1	cup butter, softened
6	large eggs
1	(8-ounce) carton sour cream
2	teaspoons vanilla extract

Nutrition Information per Serving
Serving size: 1 slice
(¹⁄₁₈ of cake)

Calories:	290
Calories from Fat:	120
Total Fat:	14g
Saturated Fat:	7g
Cholesterol:	105mg
Sodium:	120mg
Total Carbohydrate:	35g
Dietary Fiber:	0g
Sugars:	17g
Protein:	4g

Exchanges per Serving
2 Starches, 3 Fats

PREHEAT oven to 325°F.

GREASE and flour a 10-inch tube pan or a 12-cup Bundt pan; set aside.

COMBINE flour, SPLENDA® Sugar Blend and baking soda in a large mixing bowl. Cut butter into flour mixture with a fork or a pastry blender until crumbly. (This procedure may be done with a mixer at the lowest speed. Cover mixing bowl with a clean tea towel to prevent spattering.)

COMBINE eggs, sour cream and vanilla in a small mixing bowl; add ¼ of the egg mixture to flour mixture. Beat at low speed with an electric mixer until blended. Beat at medium speed for 30 seconds or until batter is smooth, stopping to scrape down sides of bowl. Repeat procedure 3 times.

SPOON batter into prepared pan.

BAKE for 1 hour and 20 minutes or until a toothpick inserted in center comes out clean. Cool in pan on a wire rack 10 minutes. Remove from pan; cool completely on a wire rack.

Meringue Bites
with Strawberries and Cream

Makes: 40 (1½-inch) meringues
Prep time: *15 minutes*
Bake time: *1 hour and 15 minutes*
Stand time: *8 hours or overnight*

Meringue
 4   egg whites
 ¼   teaspoon cream of tartar
 1   teaspoon vanilla extract
 ⅔   cup SPLENDA® Sugar Blend

Topping
 1   cup light sour cream or reduced-fat whipped topping
 40   strawberries
     Fresh mint leaves (optional)

PREHEAT oven to 250°F. Line baking sheets with parchment paper.

BEAT egg whites, cream of tartar and vanilla at high speed with an electric mixer until foamy.

ADD SPLENDA® Sugar Blend, 1 tablespoon at a time, beating until stiff peaks form and SPLENDA® Sugar Blend dissolves.

SPOON heaping tablespoonfuls of mixture onto baking sheets.

BAKE 1 hour and 15 minutes (if meringues begin to brown, reduce oven temperature to 225°F). Turn oven off. Let meringues stand in closed oven with the light on for 8 hours or overnight. Store in an airtight container.

TOP each meringue just before serving with 1 scant teaspoon of sour cream and a strawberry. Garnish with mint leaves, if desired.

Nutrition Information per Serving	
Serving size: 1 meringue	
Calories:	25
Calories from Fat:	5
Total Fat:	0g
Saturated Fat:	0g
Cholesterol:	0mg
Sodium:	10mg
Total Carbohydrate:	5g
Dietary Fiber:	0g
Sugars:	4g
Protein:	1g
Exchanges per Serving	
½ Starch	

Chocolate and Vanilla Sugar Cookies

Makes: 6 dozen cookies
Prep time: *27 minutes*
Chill time: *1 hour*
Bake time: *8 to 10 minutes*

Nutrition Information per Serving
Serving size: **2 cookies**
Calories: 130
Calories from Fat: 50
Total Fat: 6g
Saturated Fat: 3.5g
Cholesterol: 25mg
Sodium: 30mg
Total Carbohydrate: 18g
Dietary Fiber: 0g
Sugars: 7g
Protein: 2g
Exchanges per Serving
1 Starch, 1 Fat

- 3 (1-ounce) squares semisweet chocolate
- 1 cup unsalted butter, softened
- 1 cup SPLENDA® Sugar Blend
- 2 large eggs
- 2 teaspoons vanilla extract
- 4 cups all-purpose flour
- 1 teaspoon baking powder
- ¼ teaspoon salt

MELT chocolate in a 1-cup glass measuring cup on HIGH (100%) in microwave for 1 to 1½ minutes or until melted, stirring twice. Set aside.

BEAT butter at medium speed with an electric mixer in a medium mixing bowl until creamy. Gradually add SPLENDA® Sugar Blend, beating well. Add eggs, one at a time, mixing well after each addition. Stir in vanilla.

COMBINE flour, baking powder and salt in a separate mixing bowl. Gradually add flour mixture to SPLENDA® Sugar Blend mixture, beating until blended. Do not overbeat. Divide dough in half. Stir melted chocolate into half of mixture.

PLACE dough on a lightly floured work surface.

For Checker Board Cookies, shape chocolate dough into 2 rectangular logs approximately 1 inch in diameter. Repeat procedure with vanilla dough. Cut each log lengthwise into quarters. Reassemble logs, alternating chocolate and vanilla to form a checkerboard pattern. Proceed as directed below.

For Pinwheel Cookies, roll chocolate dough into 2 (8×9-inch) rectangles. Roll vanilla dough into 2 (8×10-inch) rectangles. Place vanilla layer on bottom so that it extends 1 inch beyond the chocolate layer; roll as for a jellyroll. Process as directed below.

For Striped Cookies, divide each flavor into 3 balls. Roll each ball into a 7½×3-inch rectangle; cut each rectangle into 5 (1½×3-inch strips). Stack 5 strips alternating chocolate and vanilla. Proceed as directed below.

WRAP logs in plastic wrap and chill cookie dough for one hour or until slightly firm. (Dough can be frozen up to three months at this point.)

PREHEAT oven to 350°F. Lightly grease cookie sheets.

REMOVE dough from refrigerator. Slice cookies ¼ inch thick and place on prepared cookie sheets.

BAKE 8 to 10 minutes or until edges of cookies are lightly browned. Cool slightly on cookie sheets; remove to wire racks to cool completely.

Staples

Sweet substitutes to make better meals

BBQ Sauce

Makes: about 6 cups
Prep time: *45 minutes*

Nutrition Information per Serving
Serving size: **2 tablespoons**
Calories: 20
Calories from Fat: 0
Total Fat: 0g
Saturated Fat: 0g
Cholesterol: 0mg
Sodium: 240mg
Total Carbohydrate: 4g
Dietary Fiber: 0g
Sugars: 1g
Protein: 0g
Exchanges per Serving
Free

1   tablespoon canola or extra
    virgin olive oil
1   cup onion, peeled and
    minced
2   garlic cloves, peeled and
    minced
2   low-sodium beef bouillon
    cubes
½   cup hot water
3   cans (6 ounces each) tomato
    paste
1   cup SPLENDA® No Calorie Sweetener, Granulated
¾   cup Worcestershire sauce
¾   cup Dijon mustard
3   tablespoons hickory-flavored liquid smoke
1   teaspoon salt
½   cup cider vinegar
1   tablespoon hot pepper sauce or to taste

PLACE oil in large saucepan. Add onions and garlic. Sauté over
medium heat until translucent, 2 to 3 minutes.

MIX bouillon and water. Add bouillon mixture and all remaining
ingredients to saucepan. Stir well using wire whisk.

SIMMER uncovered 25 to 30 minutes; stir often. Chill overnight in
nonreactive container to allow flavors to meld. Sauce is best if
prepared 1 day before use. Keeps for 1 week, covered in refrigerator.

"Powdered Sugar"

Makes: ½ *cup*
Prep time: 5 *minutes*

- ¾ cup SPLENDA® No Calorie Sweetener, Granulated
- 2 tablespoons cornstarch

PLACE ingredients in blender. Cover and blend until SPLENDA® Granulated Sweetener is ground into a very fine powder.

Use instead of powdered sugar to garnish cakes and pastries.

Nutrition Information per Serving	
Serving size: 1 tablespoon	
Calories:	15
Calories from Fat:	0
Total Fat:	0g
Saturated Fat:	0g
Cholesterol:	0mg
Sodium:	0mg
Total Carbohydrate:	4g
Dietary Fiber:	0g
Sugars:	0g
Protein:	0g
Exchanges per Serving	
Free	

Spicy Peanut Sauce

Makes: about 1½ *cups*
Prep time: 5 *minutes*

- ½ cup chunky or smooth peanut butter
- 2 garlic cloves, quartered
- 1 tablespoon coarsely chopped fresh ginger
- 1 small fresh hot pepper, cleaned, and diced
- ¼ cup peanut oil
- 2 tablespoons soy sauce
- 2 tablespoons SPLENDA® No Calorie Sweetener, Granulated
- 2 tablespoons rice vinegar
- 1 tablespoon sesame oil
- ¼ cup strong tea

PLACE all ingredients in food processor; purée to make sauce. Serve with chicken or noodle salad.

Nutrition Information per Serving	
Serving size: 2 tablespoons	
Calories:	120
Calories from Fat:	90
Total Fat:	11g
Saturated Fat:	2g
Cholesterol:	0mg
Sodium:	220mg
Total Carbohydrate:	3g
Dietary Fiber:	1g
Sugars:	1g
Protein:	3g
Exchanges per Serving	
½ Starch, 2 Fats	

Index

11

36

74

66

78

90